Creating Christmas Atmosphere

Creating Christmas Atmosphere

Poems of Christmas Love

by
S T KIMBROUGH, JR.

RESOURCE *Publications* • Eugene, Oregon

CREATING CHRISTMAS ATMOSPHERE
Poems of Christmas Love

Copyright © 2025 S T Kimbrough Jr. All rights reserved. Except for brief quotations in critical publications or reviews, no part of this book may be reproduced in any manner without prior written permission from the publisher. Write: Permissions, Wipf and Stock Publishers, 199 W. 8th Ave., Suite 3, Eugene, OR 97401.

Resource Publications
An Imprint of Wipf and Stock Publishers
199 W. 8th Ave., Suite 3
Eugene, OR 97401

www.wipfandstock.com

PAPERBACK ISBN: 979-8-3852-4830-8
HARDCOVER ISBN: 979-8-3852-4831-5
EBOOK ISBN: 979-8-3852-4832-2

VERSION NUMBER 05/16/25

Contents

Introduction | ix

Section 1   CHRISTMAS

1. What Do We Anticipate? | 3
2. When Advent Comes | 4
3. A Year-Round Advent | 6
4. Christmas Atmosphere | 7
5. Christmas Love | 8
6. Christmas Again | 10
7. Christmas Bells | 11
8. A Christmas Gift | 12
9. Christmas Moods | 13

Section 2   THE CHRISTMAS STORY

10. The Annunciation | 17
11. The Christmas Story | 18
12. The Age-Old Story | 19
13. Newborn Hope | 21
14. Christmas Stories | 22
15. A Christmas Story | 23
16. "Another Way" | 24

Section 3 THE HOLY FAMILY

17. The Holy Family | 27
18. Magnificat | 28
19. Mother Mary | 30
20. The Christmas Child | 32
21. The Bethlehem Child | 33
22. From Unlikely to Likely | 35
23. Christmas Security | 36

Section 4 SONGS OF CHRISTMAS

24. The Song of Christmas | 41
25. "Hark! the Herald Angels Sing" | 42
26. As We Sing the Angels' Song | 43
27. A Song of Hope and Joy | 44
28. On Christmas Morn | 45
29. Christmas Time Is Finally Here | 46

Section 5 THE MEANING OF CHRISTMAS

30. I Thought I Knew | 49
31. What Christmas Means | 50
32. Taught by a Refugee | 51
33. Humility Born Anew | 52
34. Celebrate Christmas | 53
35. A Bethlehem Walk | 54
36. Peace Within and Peace Without | 56
37. Harmony and Hope's New Start | 57
38. A Real Christmas Celebration | 58

Section 6   CHRISTMAS JOYS
- 39. It's That Time of Year | 61
- 40. Nature's Tree Ornaments | 62
- 41. A Different Christmas Tree | 63
- 42. A Holly Tree | 64
- 43. The Christmas Cactus | 65
- 44. Grandpa's Sleigh | 66
- 45. Christmas Aromas | 67
- 46. One Christmas I Remember | 68

Section 7   POST CHRISTMAS
- 47. Post Christmas | 71
- 48. The Coming of Epiphany | 72
- 49. Epiphany | 73
- 50. Revelation in the East | 74

Introduction[1]

ANOTHER CHRISTMAS BOOK! Really? Aren't there enough of them on the shelves that are taken down and thumbed through during the Christmas holidays, or that simply remain there and gather dust for another year? The answer is: Yes, another Christmas book! Although the story's content remains the same, how it is understood from year to year depends on many things: our attitudes, cultural context, geography, religion, language, music, etc. All of these influence the atmosphere we and others create and experience in and around the Christmas story and Christmas time. Perhaps one's celebration is satisfied by secular atmosphere created by "Chestnuts roasting on an open fire" or simply singing "We wish you a Merry Christmas and a Happy New Year," or that "It's the Most Wonderful Time of the Year."

Certainly nostalgia plays a role in how Christmas is celebrated and remembered. Family and cultural traditions color the atmosphere we experience. A nativity scene made by children from the Philippines may look quite different from one made by children from Zimbabwe. Nativity scenes may be surrounded by lovely decorated trees, some of which may be Chrismon trees, i.e., with handmade ornaments that depict Christian symbols. Other Christmas trees may have no reference whatsoever to the Christmas story of Holy Scripture.

---

1. The biblical quotations throughout this book are taken either from the King James Version (KJV) of the Bible or the New Revised Standard Version (NRSV). In one instance the Douay-Rheims Version (DRV) is cited.

Introduction

The decorations utilized during the Advent and Christmas seasons create an atmosphere. In particular, light and/or lights play a very significant role, be they simple white lights or colored ones. More and more we are seeing the results of digitization, whereby an image can be projected on a house or a building, or light shows that can dance to Christmas rhythms and tunes. There seems to be no limit to the kind of atmosphere, religious or secular, that can be created at the Christmas season.

This book of poems suggests images, metaphors, and words often used to celebrate and create an atmosphere for Christmas, but asks "What Do We Anticipate?" While the next-to-last section suggests, a variety of Christmas joys may or may not be specifically related to the Christmas story of a Child born in Bethlehem, they emerge from the sheer joy the season brings as one celebrates the emphasis on goodwill and peace that the Christ Child brings. Therefore, this book is written from the perspective of celebrating the birth of this Child and the message his life brings to the world desperately in need of goodwill and peace. Above all, Christmas is about love, the love God shares with all humankind in the birth of the Child Jesus, who personifies for the entire world a life of shared love. It is this shared love among peoples that brings peace and goodwill.

> Authentic Christmas atmosphere
> is simply this, and this alone:
> when healing love and peace appear
> and love in all our hearts has grown.
> When we the God-Child's love release,
> it's then that true peace can appear.
> So when we love, and we make peace,
> there is a Christmas atmosphere.

Certainly the Christmas story helps to create an atmosphere of love. It is a love story. The celebration of Christmas should be a celebration of love.

> The Bethl'hem star illuminates,
> the earth's most pow'rful force:
> a love which hate eliminates;
> sets humankind on course.

Introduction

> This love enables peace, goodwill;
>   without it we are lost.
> With Christmas love we learn the skill
>   to care at any cost.

We have many reminders of this love in church bells that chime carols that tell the story of the Bethlehem Child and his impact on lives around the world, and the need to grasp the message of peace that accompanies his birth. Whether one acknowledges it or not, each gift that is given is a reminder of the ultimate divine gift of love, peace, and goodwill in the Child whose birth we celebrate.

> Each gift, whether acknowledged so,
> reflects a gift of long ago,
> the gift of Jesus who was born
> in Bethlehem on Christmas morn.

How the Christmas story is told has much to do with the atmosphere that it creates, and we create. It can be told with stained glass, with diverse cultural images, with lyrics, melodies, rhythms. It can be told in poetry, prose, songs, and paintings. We are accustomed to those images that we find most agreeable to ourselves. Sometimes, however, we may draw images out of the Christmas story that are disturbing and stimulate us to think more deeply of its meaning. What if we should think of the Christ Child as homeless?

> A homeless child was born today;
> His mother had no place to stay.
> She found nowhere a welcome word;
> "There is no room," was all she heard.
> There was no place to lay his head,
> A mother's arms his only bed.
> There was no place to birth her boy,
> Yet angels hailed his birth with joy.[2]

It is fair to ask the question: How can we celebrate with joy the birth of a Child whose birth brings new emphasis to the

---

2. S T Kimbrough, Jr., *Rethinking Christmas*, 2020, 23.

INTRODUCTION

importance of peace in a world that is filled with enmity and hate? Where is there joy and celebration, when war rages on in diverse parts of the world?

> How can the earth with joy embrace
> a season filled with joy,
> when every moment it may face
> the threat life to destroy?

The Christmas birth emphasizes that there is hope that is larger than all human discord, but it takes commitment to selfless love and caring for which the Christ Child lived and died for such hope to have results.

> The hope we share through Jesus' birth
> transcends all hopelessness.
> Through him we know each person's worth;
> he heals our brokenness.

There is a part of the Christmas story that appears in the *Magnificat* (Luke 1:46–55) or Song of Mary that is rarely emphasized. There are many beautiful musical renderings of the *Magnificat*, the song of God's choice of the humble young woman Mary to bear the Christ Child. However, part of her song that often receives little attention addresses the reality that the powerful are brought low, the hungry are filled, and the rich go away without anything.3

> She sings that God will scatter pride,
> the powerful will be brought low,
> the lowly raised by God their Guide,
> the hungry filled, the rich must go,
> must go away without a thing.
> This is the song that Mary sings;
> this is the world the Child will bring.
> This is the world from which hope springs.

The *Magnificat* has nothing to do with "Christmas-tinsel mirth." Yet its meaning is not simply related to historical fact.

---

3. See Luke 1:52–53. "He has brought down the powerful from their thrones, and lifted up the lowly; he has filled the hungry with good things, and sent the rich away empty" (NRSV).

INTRODUCTION

> What Christmas means depends on you,
> > depends on you alone,
> for you decide if it is true
> > through peace, goodwill you've shown.

There are many ways that we learn from the Christmas story. Can we think of the Christmas Child in this manner: "A Child of peace, a refugee, / was born to set all people free"? It is a worthy question to be asked today amid the influx of refugees from many parts of the world:

> Do refugees understand best
> why everyone must love the rest,
> the rest of humankind on earth?
> Can we learn this from Jesus' birth?

In spite of the walls Israel has built today around Bethlehem, the place of Christ's birth, it is

> ... strange yet truly appropriate
> that a Palestinian boy born in Bethlehem
> lived and proclaimed a message of openness
> and caring that still lives on today,
> a message many continue to live by,
> a message that tears down man-made walls:
> "Love your neighbor, as you love yourself,"[4]
> are words he heard in the synagogue as a boy,
> and that is precisely what he did with his life.

As we celebrate the joy of Christmas, it is quite natural that our own customs and cultural affinities become a part of the celebration. They do not replace the true meaning of the joy, but rather accentuate it. Perhaps we see in these things what we want to see, especially if they are related to the meaning of Christmas. Our joys are immense and unconfined. We are delighted with the blooms of the Christmas Cactus, the aroma of mother's cooking, the pleasure of Christmas lights and decorations.

---

4. See Leviticus 19:18 and Mark 12:31, "You shall love your neighbor as yourself" (NRSV).

INTRODUCTION

With the coming of a New Year and the advent of Epiphany we tend to put away much of what is related to Christmas: old wrappings of Christmas presents, the holiday trees placed on the street for pick up, decorations carefully placed in their boxes, and crèches lovingly put away until another year.

> But Christmas I'll not put away;
> the world needs peace, goodwill.
> It needs the love born on that day.
> It needs a Savior still.

This is why we sing anew:

> O come, thou Wisdom from on high,
> and order all things far and nigh.
> To us the path of knowledge show,
> and cause us in her ways to go.5

---

5. Latin hymn; the four lines are part of a stanza of the well-known hymn "O Come, O Come, Emmanuel" translated by Henry Sloan Coffin, 1916.

Section 1
Christmas

1. WHAT DO WE ANTICIPATE?

Anticipation at Advent
    increases day by day,
yet some would like to circumvent
    what angels have to say
about a Child who's to be born,
    born into poverty,
through whom the power of death is shorn
    from us eternally.

There is no way to understand
    such an amazing birth.
Who will believe that it was planned
    by God for all on earth?
A virgin pure, Mary by name,
    gives birth to a small Child,
through whom worldwide love will acclaim,
    a love that's undefiled.

All births indeed are mysteries,
    for life begins anew,
evoking joys and miseries;
    life's plans have no preview.
And yet from Mary's newborn Child,
    a Child of peace, goodwill,
comes love by which we're reconciled,
    a love that's with us still.

2. WHEN ADVENT COMES

When Advent comes and hopes arise,
    there's reason to rejoice.
When Advent's past, it's no surprise
    that some have made the choice
the message boldly to ignore,
    ignore goodwill and peace.
How can one know what Advent's for?—
    by making both increase.

Goodwill is love in word and deed;
    it longs for peace in life
till both become our life-long creed,
    and love replaces strife.
Then Advent's meaning will be known
    in peace, goodwill made real,
a meaning everyone may own,
    and Advent's spirit *feel*.

All are the object of God's sign
    of love at Advent shown.
No one's excluded by design,
    no one is left alone.
Inclusive love is Advent's theme,
    inclusive leaves no doubt,
though often some devise a scheme
    that leaves some people out.

No one enjoys a unique claim
    to love, the love divine.
God's purpose has the highest aim:
    in Christ love to define,
a love that God with each one shares,
    with all of humankind.
The Christ Child such a love prepares,
    in him such love we find.

3. A YEAR-ROUND ADVENT

If Advent's season were year-round,
and hope and joy each day were found,
hope for a Child's birth that redeems
an evil world that crushes dreams,
would Advent be more than it seems
that stretches thoughts to bold extremes?
What if we year-round sang the songs
of peace for which the world now longs:
of neighbor-love, goodwill to all,
of helping those who stumble, fall?
If we looked for Emmanuel,
and prayed he'd come in us to dwell,
looked for his coming through the year,
then hope might live to conquer fear.

4. CHRISTMAS ATMOSPHERE

Authentic Christmas atmosphere;
   is it the sound of "Jingle Bells,"
or children's eagerness to peer
   at lights that cast their Christmas spells?

Is it "White Christmas" we hear sung
   while outside giant snowflakes fall?
Or popcorn strands so neatly strung
   round trees as we sing "Deck the hall"?

For some folk these things may be so,
   but others live in arid lands,
where food is scarce, there's never snow,
   and hunger knows but empty hands.

For others war will make no pause,
   with homes destroyed and loved ones killed.
For Jesus' birth or Santa Claus;
   on Christmas Day, who can be thrilled?

Authentic Christmas atmosphere
   is simply this, and this alone:
when healing love and peace appear
   and love in all our hearts has grown.

When we the God-Child's love release,
   it's then that true peace can appear.
So when we love, and we make peace,
   there is a Christmas atmosphere.

5. CHRISTMAS LOVE[1]

Goodwill to all and dreams of peace,
    here come these words again,
resounding from New York to Nice,
    from Norway to Bahrain.

They keep resounding year to year;
    some heed them, some ignore.
Yet every Christmas they appear,
    one asks, "So what's in store?"

In store for a world filled with rage,
    for nations waging war?
Is there no hope from age to age?
    What is each Christmas for?

Each Christmas wakens memory
    of love born in a Child.
Its star's so bright, it helps us see:
    we can be reconciled,

be reconciled by healing love
    that loves and loves again,
and gives of self, all things above,
    till all their worth regain.

---

1. Luke 2:13–14: "And suddenly there was with the angel a multitude of the heavenly host praising God and saying, Glory to God in the highest, and on earth peace, good will toward men" (KJV), or as in the NRSV, "And on earth peace among those whom he favors."

The Bethl'hem star illuminates
   the earth's most pow'rful force:
a love which hate eliminates;
   sets humankind on course.

This love enables peace, goodwill;
   without it we are lost.
With Christmas love we learn the skill
   to care at any cost.

6. CHRISTMAS AGAIN

This year under the Christmas tree,
new names the first time you will see.
The children born within the year
whose names on gifts first time appear.
It's their first Christmas, what a joy
for every newborn girl and boy.
And they replace names that we miss,
like Aunt Arlene and Uncle Chris.
For ninety-six Christmases grand
we made a circle, held a hand
of both of them with gratitude—
for every life we here include.
We're thankful for lives now not here,
for every new life bringing cheer.
This year as we hold out our hands
and make a circle, make new plans,
we offer thanks for each and all,
those who are grown, those who are small.
When Christmas comes around again
with thanks we'll sing a grand amen!

7. CHRISTMAS BELLS

The Christmas bells ring out a hymn
    of peace, but who will hear?
Those who refuse, may find life grim,
    no harmony, no cheer.

A world without the hope of peace
    has lost the hope to be,
for discord, hatred will increase
    along with enmity.

The Christmas hymn the bells have rung
    through many starlit skies,
recalls the message that was sung
    to shepherds' great surprise.

Until we listen carefully
    to these words once again
and implement them seriously,
    are Christmases in vain?

8. A CHRISTMAS GIFT

Another Christmas soon is here,
a joyous, sad time of the year.
It's joyous, for a Child is born,
who shows us love is not forlorn.
It's sad for those who've love not known,
who'll spend this Christmas all alone.

So many Christmases have past,
and yet its message seems to last.
How incomplete the quest for peace,
yet hope for goodwill does not cease.
St. Nicholas, not Santa Claus,
is someone who should give us pause.

St. Nicholas was always prone
to give gifts and remain unknown.
Such giving is a loving deed,
especially for those in need.
To give with deep humility
has greatest sensibility.

Each gift, whether acknowledged so,
reflects a gift of long ago,
the gift of Jesus who was born
in Bethlehem on Christmas morn.
Also the gift that he too gave:
his life all humankind to save.

9. CHRISTMAS MOODS

The moods of Christmas are diverse,
for some are shaped by Christmas verse,
and some when mem'ries we rehearse.
The Christmas story to traverse
means love and wonder will immerse

all those who risk to linger there
and in the Christ Child's story share.
They learn that nothing can compare
with love that hearts with peace prepare,
with goodwill which defeats despair.

We tell this story o'er and o'er,
for Christ's love new life can restore:
to those who hate life to the core,
to those who peace and good deplore,
for this he's born and even more.

Section 2

The Christmas Story

10. THE ANNUNCIATION[2]

When Gabriel came to earth to tell
    a teenage girl that she would bear
a Peace-Child named Emmanuel,
    a most unusual affair,
she did not grasp how this could be,
    but Gabriel told her not to fear.
Divine the possibility:
    God favored her, Gabriel made clear.

How overwhelming was this news;
    how overwhelming still today,
to realize that God would choose
    a mother, child to show the way:
the saving way of goodwill, peace,
    the saving way of suffering, loss,
the saving way of love's increase,
    the saving way upon a cross.

---

2. Luke 1:26–28, 30–32, "In the sixth month the angel Gabriel was sent by God to a town in Galilee called Nazareth, to a virgin engaged to a man whose name was Joseph, of the house of David. The virgin's name was Mary. And he came to her and said, 'Greetings, favored one! The Lord is with you. . . . Do not be afraid, Mary, for you have found favor with God. And now, you will conceive in your womb and bear a son, and you will name him Jesus. He will be great, and will be called the Son of the Most High, and the Lord God will give to him the throne of his ancestor David'" (NRSV).

11. THE CHRISTMAS STORY[3]

The Christmas story I first heard
    when I was very young.
I listened to each gladsome word,
    each one from father's tongue.

I was in awe of the young boy
    of whom the angels sing.
They bring to tending shepherds joy,
    for which now church bells ring.

I did not understand the king,
    King Herod was his name,
who planned to do a dreadful thing:
    to kill the boy, what shame!

I was so glad when father read
    Wise Men ignored the king,
and that the infant's family fled
    which spared God's own offspring.

I read the Christmas story now
    but see it differently.
I read the same words but somehow
    they make me wise to see,

to see through years of history
    the world is still in need
of goodwill, peace unendingly—
    God's Child still sows the seed.

3. See the accounts of the story of the birth of Jesus in Matthew 2 and Luke 2:1–19.

12. THE AGE-OLD STORY

The shepherds, Wise Men, and a king,
    unlikely characters they are,
who all three fascination bring
    with heav'nly angels and a star.

The shepherds watched on a hillside,
    attending flocks of sheep at night,
when angels sang of the Yuletide,
    the change that soon would be in sight.

Of Wise Men from the east one heard,
    how wise their interpretation.
To Herod they said not a word,
    which saved them from consternation.

This Herod, who was known as king
    and puppet of the Roman throne,
for human life cared not a thing,
    except that power was his own.

The shepherds, Wise Men we know well,
    the villain Herod we know too.
whoever will the story tell
    must surely all three keep in view.

The Wise Men faced the vanity
    of Herod's shrewd, deceptive ways,
but filled with sensibility,
    refused his wish and meet with praise.

The story's of a newborn king,
    of one who rules within the heart
and yearns not for an earthly thing,
    only for love in all to start.

13. NEWBORN HOPE

How can the earth with joy embrace
    a season filled with joy,
when every moment it may face
    the threat life to destroy?

We celebrate a child newborn,
    while one with Covid dies.
One Child with "holy" we adorn,
    another's fate: demise.

The hope we share through Jesus' birth
    transcends all hopelessness.
Through him we know each person's worth;
    he heals our brokenness.

14. CHRISTMAS STORIES

On Christmas Day a child is born,
    a healthy little girl or boy.
On Christmas Day some fam'lies mourn;
    they've lost a loved one, where's the joy?

On Christmas Day when God came down
    to earth revealed in a small Child,
the Child then bore a kingly crown
    of love by which we're reconciled.

O mystery of love's new birth
    now found in Jesus, God's own Son;
your love expresses each one's worth,
    this miracle's at Christmas done.

15. A CHRISTMAS STORY

Some Christmas stories I have heard
    are very diff'rent year by year.
Not one of them I find absurd,
    some are a thrill, others are drear.
There's just one story without change,
    which changed the course of history.
To some the story may seem strange,
    for it is filled with mystery.

Why is this story without change?
    It tells us that by peace, goodwill
we need our lives to rearrange.
    We need to hear this story still:
Both peace, goodwill now live anew
    in him, the Christ Child born this day.
For *all creation* they renew,
    and *love for all* on earth convey.

16. "ANOTHER WAY"[4]

At Advent long-awaited joy
    comes to a world losing its way,
in which King Herod sought the boy,
    the Christ Child, whom he would destroy.
The Wise Men from the East gave pause,
    and Herod's wishes set aside.
They knew his was an evil cause,
    so Herod's help the three denied.

The Wise Men went "another way,"
    would not reveal the Christ Child's place.
What wisdom did their deed convey!
    It was indeed an act of grace.
We too should go another way
    when threats to faith and life are there.
"Another way" may save the day;
    Lord, give us grace to love and dare.

---

4. Matthew 2:12, "And having been warned in a dream not to return to Herod, they left for their own country by another road" (NRSV).

Section 3

The Holy Family

17. THE HOLY FAMILY[5]

In Bethlehem a family
is working out its destiny.
It's Joseph, Mary, and a boy
(a Child whom Herod would destroy).
In Bethlehem though they're not known,
Herod the Great fears for his throne.
For soon the story's told around
of angel choirs with glorious sound
who hailed the newborn baby boy,
(the Child whom Herod would destroy).
The shepherds came in from the field,
and all before the infant kneeled.
Soon after this, the story's told
of eastern sages bringing gold,
an off'ring to the infant Child,
who's destined soon to be exiled.
Though it was said the Child brings peace,
King Herod's efforts did not cease.
He told the sages, "Bring me news,
(for Herod's desperate for clues),
so I may go and worship him."
They dared not mention Bethlehem.
The Scriptures say that God intends
in this God-Child to make amends
for human sin and enmity,
though threatened by calamity.

---

5. See Luke 2:8–20 for an account of the shepherds' visit to the newborn Jesus, the Messiah, and Matthew 2 for the account of the Wise Men and their encounter with Herod and the Christ Child.

18. MAGNIFICAT[6]

The Christmas story's filled with song.
    The Christ Child's birth was hailed by strains
of angel choirs heard ages long
    in churches, streets, or country lanes.

It's Mother Mary's song we hear,
    Magnificat, which she gives voice,
a song repeated year by year
    of thanks for God's own humble choice.

She sings that God will scatter pride,
    the powerful will be brought low.
the lowly raised by God their Guide
    the hungry filled, the rich must go,

must go away without a thing.
    This is the song that Mary sings;
this is the world the Child will bring.
    This is the world from which hope springs.

---

6. Luke 1:46–55: My soul magnifies the Lord, and my spirit rejoices in God my Savior, for he has looked with favor on the lowliness of his servant. Surely, from now on all generations will called me blessed; for the Mighty One has done great things for me, and holy is his name. His mercy is for those who fear him from generation to generation. He has shown strength with his arm; he has scattered the proud in the thoughts of their hearts. He has brought down the powerful from their thrones, and lifted up the lowly; he has filled the hungry with good things, and sent the rich away empty. He has helped his servant Israel in remembrance of his mercy, according to the promise he made to our ancestors, to Abraham and to his descendants forever" (NRSV).

They're many Christmas songs to sing:
    the joyous angel-choir refrain,
but Mary's song to all will bring
    the truths we through the Christ Child gain.

19. MOTHER MARY[7]

The Christmas carols sung each year
express a joy some love to hear.
They celebrate a gladsome birth,
that fills us with great joy and mirth.
It's easy to romanticize
a birth so many come to prize.
And yet the story's filled with woe:
the parents have no place to go!
Expectant Mary anxiously
reflects on her Child's destiny.
An innkeeper refused them space;
only a stall would be the place
where she could birth the little boy,
the source of universal joy.
An angel Mary this foretold
but not how his life would unfold.
And now in her embrace he lay,
and she would nurse him day by day.
His life begins in Mary's arms;
it's there he's sheltered from all harms.
As Mary holds him to her breast
she cannot know of the grave test
that leads to death upon a cross.
Though Pilate thought, what a great loss
to all his followers this would be,
it turned into a victory.

---

7. Mary reflected on all that she had experienced and what the shepherds shared that they had heard of the birth of her son, and "Mary treasured all these words and pondered them in her heart" (Luke 2:19, NRSV).

At her son's birth, death she was there,
the faithful mother filled with care.
She knew his life well from its start
and pondered all things in her heart.

20. THE CHRISTMAS CHILD

The Christmas Child we celebrate
    knew not the world he faced,
knew not King Herod, filled with hate
    Rome's purpose had misplaced.

The Christmas Child we celebrate
    was born a sign of peace,
was born as goodwill's advocate
    love's healing to release.

The Christmas Child we celebrate,
    must flee, the parents knew,
lest Herod should annihilate
    all boys who weren't yet two.

The Christmas Child, a refugee,
    returned, in Nazareth grew,
and in the Temple one would be
    surprised at what he knew.

The Christmas Child we celebrate
    was wise beyond his years.
He challenged leaders of the state;
    his wisdom wakened fears.

The Christmas Child we celebrate
    can make us wise as well,
if we will let him activate
    his love in us to dwell.

21. THE BETHLEHEM[8] CHILD

At Christmas time in Bethlehem,
    the town where Jesus Christ was born,
    his name his foll'wers still adorn
with songs the angels sang to them
    of peace, goodwill, yes, peace to all,
    yet round them there's been built a wall.

Yes, Bethlehem is now walled in,
    where Christians, Muslims live in peace
    and both say prayers that war will cease.
But war persists, the age-old sin,
    and hatred thrives like kudzu vines
    that choke all hope of peaceful signs.

Though one is Christian, Muslim, Jew,
    this Nazarean Jewish boy
    still has a message of great joy:
It is a life, world-changing view:
    there's nothing that can be above
    the angel's message of God's love.

The Christmas story's mystery,
    the mystery of peace, goodwill,
    a message that is needed still.
We learn that well from history,
    where hatred hinders love and peace,
    as though hate has its own police.

    8. Micah 5:2: "But you, O Bethlehem of Ephrathah, who are one of the little clans of Judah, from you shall come forth for me one who is to rule in Israel, whose origin is from of old, from ancient days" (NRSV).

The Bethl'hem Child one message brings:
    the love of self and neighbor too;
    herein we find the Christ Child's clue
to peace—it's love, not other things.
    It's love immense and unconfined;
    it's love to all of humankind.

22. FROM UNLIKELY TO LIKELY

Unlikely describes the union
of Joseph and young Mary,
who was with child but not his.
This gave Joseph sincere pause
until the *unlikely* message in a dream,
that he should take Mary as his wife.
Even more *unlikely* she was a virgin,
and with child, which was most *unlikely*.
In the synagogue, however, Joseph
had heard the prophet Isaiah's words
that a virgin would conceive and bear a son,
and he would be called Emmanuel.
Could the Child of Mary be the one
of whom the prophet Isaiah spoke?
Joseph and Mary had come to Bethlehem,
an *unlikely* place, except for its name,
beth lehem, house of bread, perhaps
a foreshadowing of her son who would
become for all peoples "the Bread of life."
Yet they were now in the most *unlikely* place
for the young mother to give birth—
in an animal stall, since no room was found.
So it was that the most *unlikely* young woman
in a most *unlikely* place gave birth to a son,
who became the most *unlikely* to proclaim
freedom to the enslaved and poor, and
justice for the unjustly imprisoned and weak.
In God's realm of justice very often
the most *unlikely* become the most *likely*.
So it was in Bethlehem centuries ago,
when Mary birthed the boy Jesus.

23. CHRISTMAS SECURITY

Security, security
    is not a Christmas word,
but purity, yes purity
    is one that we have heard
connected with the Christmas Child
    at Christmas year on year,
when God through Mary's infant smiled
    with hope that replaced fear.

Security, security
    the Holy Family feared,
and fled into obscurity
    until the threat had cleared:
that Herod was no more in power,
    and they might then return.
For Naz'reth in that trying hour
    both Mary, Joseph yearn.

Security, security,
    it's now a Christmas word,
for now it is with surety
    grave fear and *angst* have stirred.
So now there has been built a wall
    round Bethlehem of yore,
a sign of hatred's downfall,
    that spreads Christ's love the more.

The moment that love is walled-in,
    God's love abounds the more,
for love puts hatred in a spin,
    and kindness it will pour
on all—love's true security.
    For thus the Child was born:
to bring us love's maturity—
    and evil's power is shorn!

Section 4

Songs of Christmas

24. THE SONG OF CHRISTMAS[9]

The first glad tidings that we hear
    about the Christ Child's birth
are strains of song that strike the ear,
    still heard around the earth.

A bold announcement, no decree,
    no demonstrating crowd.
It is a song, sung joyfully
    with promise, hope endowed.

Emotions we feel vigorously,
    the moment that we sing,
our hearts are opened, our minds see
    new visions songs can bring.

And as we sing of Christmas night,
    of peace born in a Child,
goodwill his life's sure to ignite.
    It is as though God smiled.

God smiled on earth's chaos with love
    on every human soul,
a love we may partake thereof
    to make each person whole.

---

9. The angels' song: "Glory to God in the highest heaven, and on earth peace to people of good will" (Luke 2:14).

25. "HARK! THE HERALD ANGELS SING"[10]

I am amazed how oft I hear
a Christmas carol of good cheer
that's sung and sung year after year.

Most don't connect it with the past;
its popularity's amassed,
its author never had forecast.

Charles Wesley wrote the joyous text,
and Mendelssohn's tune was annexed,
and gladsome singing soon came next.

This carol, sung two-cent'ries long,
each year is an appropriate song
for peace, goodwill help right the wrong.

With Mendelssohn and Charles we sing,
and for the gift each year they bring,
remembrance of God's own offspring.

So, "Hark! the herald angels sing,"
and "glory to the newborn King,"
for peace to earth this Child did bring.

---

10. This is the first line of the well-known Christmas hymn by Charles Wesley (1707–1788). However, Wesley's first lines originally read, "Hark! How all the welkin rings / Glory to the King of kings." In 1753 George Whitefield (1714–1770) published a hymn book in which he changed the first two lines to read: "Hark! the herald angels sing, / Glory to the newborn king," which has survived in almost all later versions of the hymn.

26. AS WE SING THE ANGELS' SONG

As we sing the angels' song
    O what joy
    we employ,
for it lasts the ages long.

Let us praise God's Child who's born,
    who brings peace,
    love's increase,
that dwells in us night till morn.

As we sing of peace, goodwill
    we believe,
    do not grieve,
for the Child will these instill.

Instill in all who believe
    God's own love
    is above
all pow'rs on earth that deceive.

Rejoice that love's born anew:
    God's favor,
    a Savior,
a Nazarean Jew

In humility he's born
    in a stall
    for us all,
whose love leaves no one forlorn.

27. A SONG OF HOPE AND JOY

Goodwill to men and women too,
    we hear, along with dreams of peace;
and yet, who knows what we should do
    with raging wars and hate's increase?

The hope for peace, hope for goodwill
    the nations seemed then to resist,
and yet these hopes are with us still;
    somehow these hopes in us persist.

The Christmas story is a song
    we must with angels learn to sing,
a song to sing our whole lives long:
    "Goodwill and peace to you we bring."

In every culture let it ring
    and drown out choruses of hate:
"Goodwill and peace to you we bring,"
    this song is never out-of-date.

Yes, joy can overcome despair;
    it can inspire us to seek peace.
It can convince: goodwill is there;
    this song will make the joy increase.

This is a song for all to sing,
    whatever be one's faith or creed.
The Christmas Child's song, let it ring:
    Goodwill and peace all people need!

28. ON CHRISTMAS MORN

On Christmas morn, the church bells ring
reminding us that angels sing
of goodwill, peace throughout the earth;
both have new life through this Child's birth.
If there's good reason to rejoice,
shout joyfully and lend your voice.

It's time for humankind to cheer;
remove dark moods, the angry sneer.
Sing carols that proclaim goodwill,
and louder yet proclaim the thrill
of peace that's possible right now;
the Christ Child's born to show us how.

So, lift your voice in carol sings,
which every Christmas season brings,
the joyful words of Christmas cheer
and tunes so pleasing to the ear.
These sounds of joy resound each year
to celebrate that Christ is here.

29. CHRISTMAS TIME IS FINALLY HERE

Christmas time is finally here,
a joyous time year to year.
It's the time when church bells ring,
festive carols that we sing,
calling us to come and hear
the same story told each year
of a Child born in a stall
bringing peace and love to all.
Refrain:
> *Mary, Joseph, shepherds, kings,*
> *as the angel chorus sings,*
> *learn the truth of this Child's birth:*
> *spread goodwill and peace on earth.*

This is why we decorate
churches, homes, and celebrate.
This Child's name Emmanuel
is the reason that we tell
of his birth; what does it mean?
"God with us" in ev'ry scene.
This Child named Emmanuel
comes to earth with us to dwell.
Refrain:
> *Mary, Joseph, shepherds, kings,*
> *as the angel chorus sings,*
> *learn the truth of this Child's birth:*
> *spread goodwill and peace on earth.*

Section 5

The Meaning of Christmas

30. I THOUGHT I KNEW

I thought I knew what Christmas meant,
then realized how much I'd spent
to fill friends, family with cheer,
for that's what I had done last year.
How many gifts are laid aside,
because recipients won't confide:
for them some gifts just make no sense,
for which there is no recompense,
except to give them to Goodwill.
It lets them know it's Christmas still.
This year I'll send to all a note:
"Someone in need I've given a coat.
The gift this year your name will bear
to show that Christmas means to care."

31. WHAT CHRISTMAS MEANS

Events transpire in history
    and facts affirm they're true;
surround them yet with mystery
    and much depends on you.
The mystery of Jesus' birth,
    announced by angels' song,
is hailed each year around the earth
    by every Advent throng.

Believe it true, or as you will,
    this Child's birth can transform
each heart by love, and peace instill,
    and make goodwill the norm.
My friend, this will depend on you,
    depend on you alone,
for you decide if it is true
    through peace, goodwill you've shown.

32. TAUGHT BY A REFUGEE

A Palestinian family
fled into Egypt hastily.[11]
Their fear before King Herod grew,
who'd kill each male child under two.
They feared for Jesus, their own son,
through whom peace, goodwill would be won.
These he would spread across the earth.
So sang the angels at his birth.
A Child of peace, a refugee,
was born to set all people free.
By giving of himself through love,
he showed that nothing is above
love's sacrifice of self for all,
life's noblest and life's highest call.
This refugee, Jesus by name,
made love of all his central aim.
Do refugees understand best
why everyone must love the rest,
the rest of humankind on earth?
Can we learn this from Jesus' birth?

---

11. Matthew 2:13-14: "Now after they [Wise Men] had left, an angel of the Lord appeared to Joseph in a dream and said, 'Get up, take the child and his mother, and flee to Egypt, and remain there until I tell you; for Herod is about to search for the child to destroy him.' Then Joseph got up, took the child and his mother by night, and went to Egypt, and remained there until the death of Herod" (NRSV).

33. HUMILITY BORN ANEW

A humble Child of low estate
    was born humility to show,
that humankind might emulate
    humility, and then bestow
on others in their words and deeds
    a caring love that's always kind.
When humble, one will sow its seeds;
    humility's a state of mind.

Humility is born anew,
    is born anew in Bethlehem.
We've nothing of ourselves to do;
    humility, Christ's synonym.
When rooted in self-giving love,
    humility makes itself known.
Though we with joy partake thereof,
    humility you never own.

34. CELEBRATE CHRISTMAS

It's Christmas in Jerusalem;
    who'll Jesus celebrate?
Some Christians come to worship him,
    shopkeepers say, "That's great."

Though many will not welcome him,
    the Christian tourist trade
will fill its coffers to the brim
    with memorabilia that's been made.

Not just in Israel, everywhere
    Christ's birthday sets the pace
for annual economic fare,
    but meaning's hard to trace.

The temple was the place one day,
    where Jesus got it right:
Get out with all your profit play!
    Get out, get out of sight!

Yet now regardless of one's creed,
    a business prayer's like this:
"Lord, profits now we truly need,
    we trust again in Kris."

35. A BETHLEHEM WALK

I walk the streets of Bethlehem
and pass a bustling restaurant,
I see a charming Byzantine Church
which marks the place where Jesus,
at least some say, was born.
I see church buildings, minarets,
standing almost side by side.
The streets teem with tourists,
also with bustling residents.
Here Christians, Muslims live and work,
and often it seems hand in hand.
Left and right are souvenir shops,
some filled with busy tourists
searching for the right souvenir
to commemorate their long-awaited,
perhaps only, trip to the Holy Land.
Suddenly the street stops; I can't go on.
A giant wall stands high before me.
A dead end street? I can't continue.
Each day the residents face this wall;
they cannot go a step further.
The wall was built to keep
the Palestinians separate.
Checkpoints mark entrances, exits
to the occupied area round Bethlehem,
much like the Warsaw Jewish ghetto.
There's no other way to enter or leave.
Bethlehem is an enclosed, walled-in city.
I turn, walk back to my hotel thinking—
How strange yet somehow appropriate

that a Palestinian Jewish boy, born in Bethlehem,
lived and proclaimed a message of openness
and caring that still lives on today.
It's a message many continue to live by,
a message that tears down man-made walls.
"Love your neighbor as you love yourself,"[12]
are words he heard in the synagogue as a boy,
and that is precisely what he did with his life.

---

12. See Leviticus 19:18 (and Mark 12:31), "Love your neighbor, as you love yourself" (NRSV).

36. PEACE WITHIN AND PEACE WITHOUT

We sing of peace at Christmas time,
    yet there's no peace on earth.
We search the nations, every clime
    for peace hailed at Christ's birth.

Are we to peace within consigned;
    is there no peace without?
Are we to war, conflict consigned,
    for world peace only doubt?

Peace must begin in everyone,
    in all must coincide.
It's then the first steps have begun—
    the peace of Christmastide.

37. HARMONY AND HOPE'S NEW START

Whenever Advent comes again,
    I'm filled with disappointment, joy,
for worldwide peace there's little gain,
    and many would goodwill destroy,
but Advent keeps the hope alive
    that peace can reign within a heart,
so that among all hearts we'll strive
    for harmony and hope's new start.

For ages some folk dare believe
    that every Advent marks the birth
of one through whom we may perceive
    a love that spreads across the earth.
Embraced by love, the little Child
    embraces all of humankind:
the rich, the poor, and the defiled
    with mercy, love, and grace combined.

38. A REAL CHRISTMAS CELEBRATION

What of the child at Christmas time
    who cannot sing for joy,
knows neither Christmas bells nor rhyme,
    nor Mary's baby boy?

She has no parents, Christmas tree;
    she's not heard "Silent Night."
Her brother's blind and cannot see;
    their lives are a sad plight.

What diff'rence to them should it make
    that Christ the Lord is born?
Can they know he's born for their sake,
    or they are left forlorn?

Sing on, sing on "Joy to the world,"
    for each forsaken child.
Let joy for each one be unfurled,
    the joy of the God-Child.

So let us Christmas celebrate,
    bring joy where it's unknown.
This will its meaning demonstrate,
    for "goodwill" we'll have shown.

Section 6

Christmas Joys

39. IT'S THAT TIME OF YEAR

Wherever Christmas lights appear,
    come changes in the air:
a lighter step this time of year,
    a willingness to share.

On city corners old St. Nick
    rings bells for charity,
for generosity's uptick,
    and less temerity.

But seasonal generosity
    should find a year-round pace,
replaced by regularity,
    warm welcome on each face.

40. NATURE'S TREE ORNAMENTS

The pine cones hanging on a tree
    are dusted lightly with soft snow.
Exquisitely they dangle there,
    by someone who is "in the know."

Amid a grove of blue spruce trees
    the pine tree has a Christmas charm.
Each passerby it seems to please
    at Christmas on grandpa's tree farm.

The white-tipped pine cones aren't for sale.
    They're Mother Nature's own design,
decor you can't get through the mail.
    Their quality's first-rate, just fine.

41. A DIFFERENT CHRISTMAS TREE

How green the evergreens year round,
I need not their green hues expound.
They are some forests' year-round stay,
a frequent joy on Christmas day.
For Christmas trees a regal pine?
No, I prefer blue firs for mine.
My mother said on Christmas Eve,
a tale I found hard to believe.
Her father brought a holly tree
into their house for all to see,
to decorate with popcorn strands,
but how they had to watch their hands.
For more than once the prickly leaves
did prick her arms right through her sleeves.
But berries red and leaves of green
made such a perfect Christmas scene.
Perhaps this year a holly tree
would be a perfect memory
of mother and her father too.
Yes, this year that's what I should do.

42. A HOLLY TREE

A holly tree with berries red
    adorns my yard the year around,
and of the holly tree it's said,
    there's symbolism in it found.

For many, colors red and green
    are part of Christmas-time decor,
and everywhere they can be seen.
    For others there is more in store.

Its sharply-pointed leaves of green
    remind one of the crown of thorns
upon Christ's head that once was seen
    and of his tragic fate forewarns.

The color red recalls the blood
    that Christ shed on a wooden cross.
His sacrifice released a flood
    of selfless love that knows no loss.

The holly berries first are green,
    in season they will turn to red.
The green of growth must first be seen
    so berries turn to red instead.

Like holly berries one must grow,
    just as they turn from green to red:
Self-giving love one comes to know
    when following Christ, the Loving Head.

43. THE CHRISTMAS CACTUS

The Christmas cactus in my room
knows that it's time for it to bloom.
It's winter, near to Christmas time,
when pink, its blooms are in their prime.
Though dormant so much of the year,
near Christmas charming flow'rs appear.
We humans often tend to be
like Christmas cactuses we see:
we let our beauty dormant lie,
and no one understands just why!
Let others your own beauty see,
but let them see it constantly.

44. GRANDPA'S SLEIGH

When snow falls day by day
and clouds are cast in gray,
it's time to bring out grandpa's sleigh,
and hear its bells resound
as horses outward bound.
We climb in and we ride away.

The ground is packed with snow
as round a curve we go.
Then suddenly a large oak tree
decked out in winter white,
lies fallen, what a sight.
The horses stopped immediately.

It fully blocked the trail,
no need for each detail.
"There is another way to go,"
grandpa joined in to say,
"Go left down by the bay;
right through the woods where you'll see snow."

Our pace was very slow,
because of drifts of snow.
Then all at once before our eyes
we saw a horse-trod trail,
which was our holy grail,
for it then made us home-bound wise.

45. CHRISTMAS AROMAS

Some fruitcake and some peppermint,
    some red-green cookies and mince pie,
perhaps will give you a slight hint—
    a holiday is very nigh.

The gingerbread my mother made,
    the cider seasoned with fresh cloves,
aromas that don't quickly fade,
    were some of mother's treasure troves.

The kitchen was the place to be;
    I hoped to taste each festive dish.
When empty bowls were passed to me,
    my mother knew my every wish.

Around inside a bowl I'd go,
    my fingers capturing a taste
of gingerbread-mix I loved so,
    and not a bit would go to waste.

Ambrosia was a special treat,
    but rarely was a foretaste giv'n.
The fruit must stay all fresh and sweet;
    so eager fingers weren't forgiven.

I would not trade these memories
    for all the Christmas treats you buy.
My mom's kitchen festivities,
    gave me a Christmas all-time high!

46. ONE CHRISTMAS I REMEMBER

One Christmas I remember well,
    High in the Swiss Alps where
in early morning you could tell
    the snow would soon be there.

The day before we'd had snow too
    and filmed a Christmas show
with Christmas carols that I knew,
    and sleigh rides in the snow.

The camera man, a happy sort,
    laughed just like Ol' Saint Nick.
He let not one scene come up short;
    he seemed to know each trick.

One sleigh scene needed two reindeer,
    but there was only one,
and so we asked, "Is Nick not here?
    "Where's Rudolph? On the run?"

We filmed the one-horse driven sleigh,
    as we sang "Silent Night."
The horse then added one loud NEIGH,
    and we were out of sight.

Section 7

Post Christmas

47. POST CHRISTMAS

The ornaments are put away,
    the tree lights neatly packed,
the stockings no more on display,
    the pine needles are sacked.

The Christmas candle grandma made
    won't burn until next year.
Last year its scent just stayed and stayed,
    a source of Christmas cheer.

The Christmas tree lies on the street;
    recycling will be soon.
Then nature's cycle is complete:
    it helps build a sand dune.

But Christmas I'll not put away;
    the world needs peace, goodwill.
It needs the love born on that day.
    It needs a Savior still.

48. THE COMING OF EPIPHANY

The coming of Epiphany
recalls the great theophany
when Wise Men from the east once came
to honor One unknown by name:

appearance of the Child divine
whose birth would be a sacred sign,
a sacred sign of peace, goodwill,
and love inclusive to instill,

instill in all across the earth,
"God with us," present through his birth.
Emmanuel, ever his name,
"God with us," always to proclaim.

A wondrous star brought Wise Men hence
with gifts of gold, myrrh, frankincense.
They knelt before the Child in awe
with gifts Isaiah of old foresaw.

If sages chose to honor him,
how wise that we now sing a hymn[13]
that celebrates that sages came
the Child as royal to acclaim.

---

13. See "We three kings of orient are," words and music by John H. Hopkins (1857).

49. EPIPHANY

A festival's observed today
to celebrate a different way
the Christmas story is made known,
how sharing of its truth has grown.
For Wise Men from a distant land
through ancient wisdom understand
a star will guide them to a birth
that spreads a love across the earth,
much more than even these Wise Men
had known for ages until then.
Epiphany reminds us all
that love is greater, said St. Paul,
is greater than both faith and hope.
That's why each year we sing the trope:
"O come, thou Wisdom from on high,
and order all things far and nigh.
To us the path of knowledge show,
and cause us in her ways to go."[14]

---

14. Latin hymn; the four lines are part of a stanza of the well-known hymn "O Come, O Come, Emmanuel" translated by Henry Sloan Coffin, 1916.

50. REVELATION IN THE EAST

A revelation in the east
    brought Wise Men to a distant place,
a place where they would find the least,
    a Child who'd fill the world with grace.

Since then from north, south, east, and west
    millions have journeyed to the Child
to learn from ancient Wise Men's quest
    how people might be reconciled.

If you are wise, you bow before
    the child, whose love for everyone,
gives all of self the more and more,
    the pathway of th' Almighty's Son.

The reconciling love he shared
    was caring and forbearing, wise;
and to the entire world declared:
    the love of others is the prize.

Yes, those who serve the living God
    are selfless, they delight to give.
The path of goodwill, peace they trod,
    and practice both long as they live.

This is a great epiphany,
    the opening of the heart and mind,
a vision, a theophany,
    the life and love for humankind.

www.ingramcontent.com/pod-product-compliance
Lightning Source LLC
Chambersburg PA
CBHW061500040426
42450CB00008B/1435